GOSPEL LESSONS FROM MY

HEROES

JAMES D. HOLT

ISBN 13: 978-1-4621-4104-3

Published by CFI, an imprint of Cedar Fort, Inc.
2373 W. 700 S., Springville, UT 84663
Distributed by Cedar Fort, Inc., www.cedarfort.com

Printed in the United States of America

10 9 8 7 6 5 4 3 2 1

Printed on acid-free paper

CFI
An imprint of Cedar Fort, Inc.
Springville, Utah

GOSPEL LESSONS FROM MY

HEROES

JAMES D. HOLT

Dedicated to my mum who introduced me to the world of fantasy and to the Restored Gospel of Jesus Christ.

Acknowledgements

Always my thanks go to Ruth, Eleanor, Abi, Ethan, Gideon and Martha who inspire me each day.

Also thanks to Rob Schwartz, Beth Teal and Jacob Teal who read drafts and made comments that immeasurably improved this work. Needless to say, any mistakes remain mine; these are much less because of your contributions. Most importantly, my Heavenly Father, Saviour Jesus Christ and the Holy Ghost. Without them I would be nothing. They have created, and continue to redeem and sustain me. These are debts I can never repay.

Gospel Lessons from My Heroes

INTRODUCTION

I have a number of loves in my life. First and foremost is my Saviour Jesus Christ; without Him I would be nothing. I suppose I would not even be. After my family, not to gloss over them too quickly, comes the devotion and relationship I have with my religion. As a member of the Church of Jesus Christ of Latter-day Saints my character, choices and personality are shaped, in large manner, by the religious beliefs I hold. One of my further loves, though not to the same degree, is my love of fantasy literature, science-fiction in all its forms, and comic books. It is a way that I relax but it is also a way that I learn.

For a long time, my relationship with my Saviour and my interest in the world of fantasy were completely separate. I didn't see how one could help the other. At certain points I convinced myself that my interest in fantasy was one of those "childish things" that Paul warned I should "put away" (1 Corinthians 13:11). When it came to my comic books, I literally put them away into a box in the garage, though I have to admit I still watched the science fiction and superhero films that I had grown to love. Then I had children and rediscovered a whole new world of through Tolkien, elements of Narnia, the Fablehaven chronicles, and the resurgence of Marvel and DC universe films. I read or reread these to be aware of what my children were engaging with.

In the midst of my children growing up and becoming teenagers, I was studying for a PhD in my spare time. These studies didn't have anything to do with comic books and fantasy but focussed around the possibility of religious people learning from other people's religious experiences. The conclusion I came to was that I could learn deeper things about my own faith as I engaged with people who held different beliefs. I think dialogue between two people is incredibly important as it helps each learn more about the other and what they believe, and it also helps me personally to learn more about myself and why I believe the things that I do.

What does this have to do with fantasy, science fiction and comic books? All of these are stories that I think can help us learn more about ourselves as we engage with them. In my work as a University Professor I teach those who are training to be teachers. In preparing them to teach Religious Education I explore the importance of stories in helping people understand religious concepts. We explore the parables of Jesus, the stories of his miracles, and we also explore the epics of the Ramayana and the Bhagavad Gita from Hinduism and many other stories from the religious world. We also explore the importance of modern stories; stories about people who live today to help us understand the impact that faith can have on people's lives. Through all of this we begin to realise that just as we have relationships with other people, we can also have relationships with the stories we hear, watch and read.

Engaging with story in all its forms is potentially transformative. Utilising such stories can enhance our experience of a person's faith and worldview. Gordon B. Hinckley suggested that in encounters with people of other religions members should "Look for their strengths and virtues, and you will find strengths and virtues in your own life" (in Dew, 1996: 576). I think that the finding of virtues will come in the encounter between us and the stories that we read. We can't help being changed by engaging with story.

In the English Literature lessons I remember from school we had to explore what the author meant in a particular passage, poem or book. While that is important, when I think about my reading of stories it is much more important to consider what I can take from them. In reading stories in this way, the intention of the author is secondary to the experience of the reader. Philip Pullman has suggested:

> ***"As a passionate believer in the democracy of reading, I don't think it's the task of the author of a book to tell the reader what it means. The meaning of a story emerges in the meeting between the words on the page and the thoughts in the reader's mind. So when people ask me what I meant by this story, or what was the message I was trying to convey in that one, I have to explain that I'm not going to explain" (2015).***

Orson Scott Card (a science fiction writer and a member of the Church) has suggested that:

> ***"Fictional storytelling is particularly powerful, however, because the author invites the audience to live inside the world of the story and add the events of the story to their own memories as if they had lived them. Of course, audience***

members filter and edit the stories they receive. Things that to the author or other readers might be unnoticed will make a much deeper impression on a particular reader, because of his own concerns or experiences. Readers bring their own attitudes to the stories they are given; what seems obvious and important to one might seem trivial or non-existent to another " (2010).

How we respond to what we read, listen to, and watch is important in developing who we are. As a teenager my life was changed by reading two books; the first was The Book of Mormon, and the second was To Kill a Mockingbird. Both of these books changed the way that I viewed myself and the world. Obviously, The Book of Mormon has more importance for eternity, but the things I learned from To Kill a Mockingbird about the equality of all people and the importance of treating others fairly, fed into the way that I lived the Gospel and made (and make) me a better person.

Why have I spent so long in a book about heroes talking about the importance of stories? I think it's important that we realise that as we experience these stories through whatever medium, we should be open to learning. We could even suggest that the reading of these books about heroes is a part of the Lord's plan for us. In the Doctrine and Covenants, the Lord implores:

And as all have not faith, seek ye diligently and teach one another words of wisdom; yea, seek ye out of the best books words of wisdom; seek learning, even by study and also by faith (D&C 88:118).

I believe these stories, along with many others, are some of these 'best books' because they teach me more about my Saviour and my relationship with Him. We just need to be open to learning.

In this book I am going to talk about what I have learned from some of my heroes in the world of fantasy. Some may not be your heroes, but their stories and what you can learn from them are for you to discover. Please remember that my responses to these stories and the things that I learn from them are probably not what the author intended but that doesn't matter. They have helped me understand some Gospel principles and that is what I am going to share. The heroes we will learn from are Superman, the Black Panther (and Shuri), Elphaba, and Samwise Gamgee.

There are many characteristics in the life and times of Superman that have led me in many different directions. I still remember watching the

SUPERMAN

very first Superman film in my local cinema and being mesmerised by his heroism and his fight for 'Truth, Justice and the American Way'. I'm not sure what the American Way is, but as a five-year-old the film filled my imagination with excitement. There have been many developments in the life and character of Superman in the intervening years, some good (I love Smallville) and others not so (Batman v Superman). One that sticks out in my mind is the Man of Steel film that reimagined the sending of Kal-El to earth by his parents, Jor-El and Lara Lor-Van. As they place him into the ship that will carry him to earth the voiceover is heard:

Lara: ***He'll be an outcast. They will kill him.***
Jor-El: ***How? He will be a god to them.***

It's possible that the writers were drawing on an archetype from history, but I think the filmmakers purposefully used this Saviour motif to show echoes of the Christian story. It has direct links to the prophecies about Jesus Christ:

"For he shall grow up before him as a tender plant, and as a root out of a dry ground: he hath no form nor comeliness; and

when we shall see him, there is no beauty that we should desire him. He is despised and rejected of men; a man of sorrows, and acquainted with grief: and we hid as it were our faces from him; he was despised, and we esteemed him not. Surely he hath borne our griefs, and carried our sorrows: yet we did esteem him stricken, smitten of God, and afflicted" (Isaiah 53:2-4).

The parallel can only be taken so far. Throughout the comic books and films Superman is seen to be a great hero with few, if any, detractors. The same could not be said about the life of Jesus. Undoubtedly, He is a hero, but He was rejected and ultimately killed by those who opposed him. Although He had the power of God, he chose to lay His life down willingly to save humanity:

"No man taketh it from me, but I lay it down of myself. I have power to lay it down, and I have power to take it again. This commandment have I received of my Father (John 10:18)."

In this way Jesus can be seen to be a greater hero as he recognised the inevitability and necessity of his death in order for humanity to ultimately live again. With every confrontation that Superman entered into, death was a possibility but was never assured, and I assume he went in thinking/hoping that he would survive. I am very conscious that there may be some Superman experts out there who are shouting at the book: 'But, Superman did die!' Indeed, he did, I have the graphic novel The Death of Superman that includes the three original stories of Doomsday, Funeral for a Friend, and Reign of the Supermen. In these books Superman dies at the hands of Doomsday and is ultimately regenerated and regains his powers. I am sure I could make some links to the death and resurrection of the Saviour, but in my reading my mind never really took me in that direction, but that's not to say it won't do at some future point.

The element of Superman and his stories that has had most impact on me in the way that I live the Gospel is the relationship between Clark Kent and Superman. In all of the stories of Superman that I have either read or watched, Superman has had to hide his identity in everyday life as the bespectacled Clark Kent (as though a pair of glasses and different hairstyle is likely to fool anyone- though it worked for Hannah Montana too!). He even adopts mannerisms and character traits that are the complete opposite of Superman – Clark is often bumbling, uncoordinated and nervous. To protect his secret and allow his secret identity to be preserved this double life becomes an important part of who he is, reinforced by his well-meaning parents (Jonathan and Martha) since his childhood.

How does this apply to us? Sometimes we might try and separate aspects of our lives: we might think this is the James I am at work, this is who I am at home, and this is who I am at Church. There are overlaps but sometimes we might accentuate certain of our characteristics or hide some of our values. I think back to my life as a teenager, having just joined the Church. In certain situations, I pretended to be less obedient than I was. This may seem odd, I wasn't doing anything wrong but I was suggesting I might not be as settled in heart as to the Gospel. Elder Neal A. Maxwell suggested this kind of attitude is wrong:

> ***"While casual members are not unrighteous, they often avoid appearing to be too righteous by seeming less committed than***

they really are—an ironic form of hypocrisy (1992)."

Maybe we can all do this from time to time, but pretending to be less than we are does not serve anybody well, and certainly does not serve the Saviour.

Let me share another personal experience from when I was applying to a teacher training course. I had applied in the last year of my undergraduate degree, and the time I had spent on my mission was on the application. I was asked, 'How will your faith affect you in the classroom? 'I did not react as I now think I should have but I did ask for clarification. The interviewer explained, '

Surely your faith requires you to witness within the classroom?'

I pointed out that my faith would not affect me in the classroom. In the intervening years I have had cause on numerous occasions to reflect on the answer I gave. For the first few years, I was happy with the righteous indignation I had shown – my faith would not affect me in the classroom. This was my Clark Kent persona, somewhere hidden behind my role as a teacher was my faith in the Lord Jesus Christ. My career and my faith were separate and never the twain would meet. The questions continued from people within and outside the Church:

'How could I, as a Latter-day Saint, teach RE?"

I eventually came to the conclusion that my initial reaction, and the first few years of not seeing the influence my faith had in the classroom, were wrong. Despite my denials, my faith was an integral part of my classroom practice.

One of my favourite quotes is from President Howard W. Hunter which echoes the teaching of Jesus to 'Come, follow me' (Luke 18: 22):

"I would invite all members of the Church to live with ever more attention to the life and example of the Lord Jesus Christ, especially the love and hope and compassion He displayed. I pray that we might treat each other with more kindness, more courtesy, more humility and patience and forgiveness (Hunter, 1994, p. 14)."

If I explore what lies behind this invitation I am led to the experiences of the life of Jesus; whether it is when he was moved with compassion to raise the son of the Widow of Nain, when he blessed the little children, or when he bore the pains and humiliation of the cross with grace and love for all people. This teaching builds on the belief that every person is a child of God. As such, I should treat every person or every child in my classroom in the way that Jesus would. He would not turn any away because of the way that they looked (the woman anointing his feet with oil), what they had done in the past (the woman caught in adultery), or how they treated him (he died for all of humanity even those who nailed him to the cross). Am I fulfilling the command to ***'strengthen [everyone] in all your conversation, in all your prayers, in all your exhortations, and in all your doings' (D&C 108:7)?***

I must build up every child whom I teach in every aspect of my dealings with them, I must not lose patience when they stretch it to breaking point, I must offer time and understanding. Every year as I address a new group of trainee teachers I offer my philosophy of teaching which is to

'be the kind of teacher I want my own children to have'

which is only a slightly disguised plagiarism of the Golden Rule. For me, as a Latter-day Saint, I must follow Jesus' example in every aspect of my life. The command to follow him was not a part-time exhortation. By acknowledging their influence on my teaching practice, I can live a more cohesive life where I don't have to separate aspects of my personality and identity. I am a teacher and I am also a Latter-day Saint. This does not mean that I preach my faith in the classroom, just that I live it as best as I can.

Just as there are many problems in the living of two lives by Clark Kent and Superman, so we must have a unified approach to our lives as disciples of Jesus Christ. We need to be every day, every moment disciples of Jesus Christ rather than weekend warriors who use the armour of God as a bolt on and bolt off accessory. In every area of our lives; in school, in work, in our homes, in our chapels, we have covenanted to stand as a witness of Him. We cannot and should not pretend to be something we are not; it will only bring frustration if we can't truly be ourselves.

We cannot and should not pretend to be something we are not; it will only bring frustration if we can't truly be ourselves.

I have to admit that my first experience of The Black Panther was in the Marvel films; his wasn't a comic book that I had read. As such, there

BLACK PANTHER & SHURI

may be many elements of his background that I don't engage with, and the representation of him that I will explore will based mainly on the film. In light of this discussion of T'Challa I will also make mention of his younger sister, Shuri (though it should be recognised that her role in the comics is much larger and more interesting).

As King of Wakanda and as the Black Panther, T'Challa is tasked with the protection of his people, and of the secret of vibranium that enables his society and his people to prosper, all the while hiding it from the outside world. There are many aspects of T'Challa and his personality that could be explored in terms of being springboards for helping me better understand my living of the Gospel of Jesus Christ. For example, his turning away from seeking vengeance for the death of his father to enable him to return home to fulfil his duty and care for his people. His discussion of death is similarly inspiring:

In my culture, death is not the end. It's more of a stepping off point. You reach out with both hands and Bast and Sekhmet, they lead you into a green veld where you can run forever.

The idea of a stepping off point has such resonance as we think of the place of death in the plan of salvation. Death is not the end, it is merely a new beginning in a different sphere, but all of life including the pre-mortal existence, mortality and life after death are aspects of the eternity in which we are living. In the words of Elder Neal A. Maxwell,

> ***"death is a mere comma, not an exclamation point!"** (1983, "**Shine As Lights in the World**"), **the sentence will continue.***

I think one of the things that strikes me most about T'Challa is his courage and his compassion. These are not mutually exclusive. Throughout the film I often wondered at the technology of the Wakandans, and perhaps purposefully on the part of the filmmakers was left to wonder why such advancements that benefitted Wakandan society were not made widely available. Prior to his death, T'Challa's uncle desired to share the technology as a way for black people around the world to throw off the shackles of oppression. As I watched Shuri use Wakandan technology to heal CIA agent Everett Ross it was evident that we were supposed to wonder at such technology and recognise elements of the insular thought process that kept it solely in Wakandan hands.

The whole film seems to lead to the scene at the end where Shuri is the instigator of the need to share the knowledge and technology of the Wakandans. It is for this reason that Shuri is included in the title to this section; it is at her prompting that T'Challa is able to see the inevitable. Sometimes we need the sensitive insight of others to give us a nudge in the right direction. Despite the concerns of some of the people in the United Nations about what Wakanda can offer, T'Challa makes the statement in his address that:

"Wakanda will no longer watch from the shadows. We cannot. We must not. We will work to be an example of how we, as brothers and sisters on this earth, should treat each other. Now, more than ever, the illusions of division threaten our very existence. We all know the truth: more connects us than separates us. But in times of crisis the wise build bridges, while the foolish build barriers. We must find a way to look after one another as if we were one single tribe."

There is so much in just this one passage that sends me in lots of directions with regards to the Gospel. I begin to think of the technology that Wakandans were able to develop from vibranium which would enable the world to flourish. At a much deeper level, it is not technology that will bring the world together or 'save' the world, but greater love. More importantly more Christlike love being shown. In a way similar to the Wakandans, members of the Church of Jesus Christ can often find themselves becoming insular and looking after themselves. Don't get me wrong, self-care is important and there is an injunction in the scriptures that we are to learn and develop ourselves in terms of the Gospel principles before we share them. Hyrum Smith desired to preach the Gospel and received this revelation from the Lord:

"Seek not to declare my word, but first seek to obtain my word, and then shall your tongue be loosed; then, if you desire, you shall have my Spirit and my word, yea, the power of God unto the convincing of men" (D&C 11:21).

Once we have obtained the word

"it becometh every man who hath been warned to warn his neighbour" (D&C 88:81).

As disciples of Jesus Christ we are called to be "the salt of the earth" (Matthew 5:13). I once heard a sacrament talk that suggested we can't fulfil our purpose as the salt to savour the earth if we are clumped together in the cultural hall. There is a responsibility for all of us to be outward looking and share the fundamental truths of the Gospel so that the whole world can be blessed.

You may be thinking that this is obvious. We are a missionary-oriented Church, we have thousands of young people (and many older couples) around the world sharing the message of the Gospel, but this doesn't take away our individual responsibility to share the Gospel. Firstly, when the opportunity comes for us to serve a mission we should enthusiastically serve. Prophets have told young men that this is their Priesthood responsibility, and for young women it is their choice. Even with this prophetic counsel we can sometimes question if a mission is for us. I remember as a seventeen-year-old deciding that I needed to pray to see if I should serve a mission (I thought I should but wanted the confirmation of the Lord). It is not very often that I audibly hear an answer to my prayer, but this time I did, and it said: "I have told you through my Prophet, what other answer do you need?" There are even greater opportunities today, including for those who would previously have been unable to serve, with the worldwide introduction of Church service missionaries.

Our responsibility is not just to serve a mission but to be missionaries every day of our life. Elder Neal A. Maxwell suggested:

"Will we do the same… by witnessing to our families, friends, and flocks—not only through our verbal testimonies but also by our developmental examples? We can do this by becoming ever more visibly the men [and women] of Christ!" (1992a).

We are to be in our communities and nations sharing the Gospel and the influence of the Saviour in all areas of our lives, not just in our relationships with other members. We live the Gospel of Jesus Christ in every facet of our lives so that, while recognising that we will fall, we can radiate the light of Christ in our lives. St Francis of Assisi is reported to have said (though he probably didn't): "Preach the gospel at all times; when necessary, use words." Being a disciple of Christ is a lot about who we are, what we do in addition to what we believe. We can be described as was John the Baptist:

"The same came for a witness, to bear witness of the Light, that all men through him might believe. He was not that Light, but was sent to bear witness of that Light. That was the true Light, which lighteth every man that cometh into the world." (John 1: 7-9).

We should not become stumbling blocks to the Gospel of Jesus Christ:

"the wickedness of the church was a great stumbling-block to those who did not belong to the church; and thus the church

began to fail in its progress." (Alma 4:10).

My faith and religion permeate every aspect of my life. As a parent I strive to follow the patience and love that my Saviour showed. As a friend I try to exemplify the service that Jesus taught and showed. In my recreational time I try and abide by the teachings of the Saviour and the prophets, such that there are many films I will not watch, music I will not listen to and substances I will not use. In my career, my faith is an integral part of who I am. In my relationships with others I strive to eliminate any form of prejudice, and seek to champion the rights of all people, especially those who could be described as being in a minority.

Sometimes we are guilty of living in echo chambers, places where all we hear are voices like our own. We are called to be disciples of Jesus Christ and witness to the whole world. We can't do this if we don't step outside of our chapels. We have a responsibility, as part of the Abrahamic Covenant, to bless all nations. We can't hide as the Wakandans did in blissful joy behind an invisible shield. We stand and share our testimonies through the way that we live and the organisations and projects we support and become both the salt which provides savour to the world, and the light which is set on the hill as we point the way to the Saviour.

Elphaba is maybe the least well known of the 'heroes' that I'm exploring in the booklet. She is perhaps better known by her original description

You are what you
choose to become

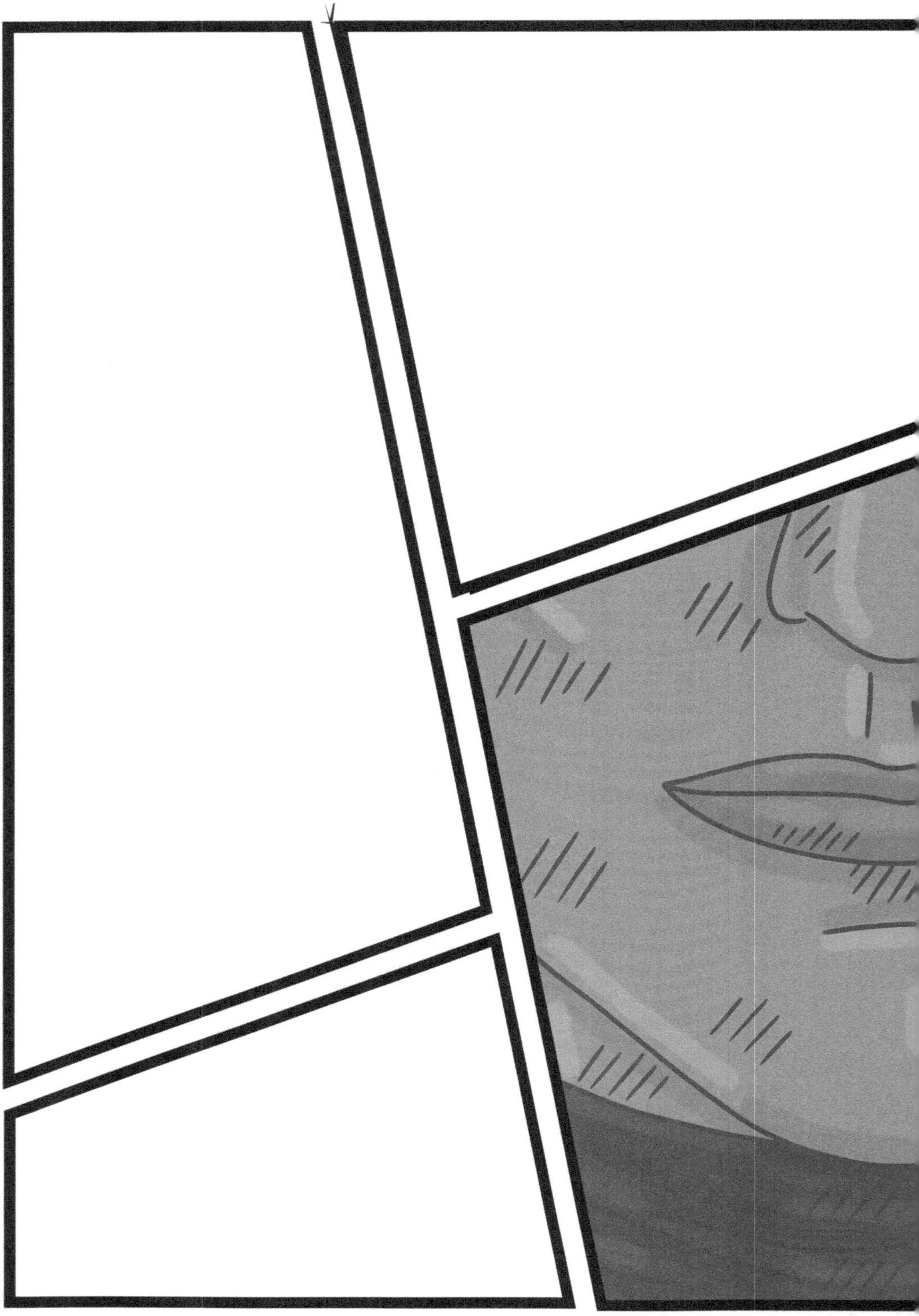

Elphaba

in L. Frank Baum's The Wizard of Oz: The Wicked Witch of the West. The story of Dorothy and her companions was reimagined by Gregory Maguire, and then latterly on the stage in Wicked: The Life and Times of the Wicked Witch of the West. It may seem strange in a discussion that seems to focus on comic book and film characters to choose someone who is best known from musical theatre, but from her I have been inspired in different ways to live the Gospel just that little bit better, and to become more Christlike in my discipleship.

When we read or watch the original Wizard of Oz the picture that we are presented of the Wicked Witch of the West is very one dimensional, in that she is evil personified. The presentation of Elphaba in Wicked is much more nuanced. There are elements of her character and actions that are bad, but that doesn't necessarily make her a bad person. I am reminded of the line from Wreck-it-Ralph where one person is ruminating on the complexity of his character:

"You are bad guy, but this does not mean you are bad guy."

She is someone who is trying to do her best. Elphaba's actions lead me to consider how I could better live as a disciple of Jesus Christ.

The Wizard in the original book is seen to be a fraud, but it would appear a well-meaning one who just got caught up in the moment. In Wicked, while he is the same person from our world he is also seen to be a character of a much more dangerous nature. As ruler of Oz he is seen to be an oppressive and callous leader. The most obvious example of this is in his treatment of the Animals (the A is capitalised to differentiate between the sentient Animals who are able to think and other animals who are not). In the song 'Something bad is happening in Oz' Elphaba talks with her history professor, Dr Dillamond, who is a Goat. They talk about reports of the oppression of Animals, with some being removed from teaching posts and others losing the ability of teach. The denial of sentience and rights to Animals is horrendous to Elphaba. She can't countenance that such an event is happening and that the great Wizard cannot know of such a thing, and thinks someone should tell him.

There are many aspects of these and the resultant events that give me pause, and help me consider my responses to injustices and the living of the Gospel of Jesus Christ. Elphaba is not directly affected by the policies or the injustices that are being endured by Animals but she is motivated to action. Sometimes I can sit in the safety of my circumstances and pretend nothing is happening, or that the events in my community, wider society, and the world are of no concern to me because they don't affect me. This isn't the point, if I see social inequality or injustice, as a disciple of Jesus Christ I should respond in an Elphaba-like way. We can consider the Parable of the Sheep and Goats in Matthew 25 where the Saviour declares:

"Verily I say unto you, Inasmuch as ye have done it unto one of the least of these my brethren, ye have done it unto me." (verse 40).

Perhaps verse 45 is more sobering as the Saviour declares the opposite; that if we didn't feed the hungry or clothe the naked it is as though we ignored Him. There are elements of this parable that find their expression in King Benjamin's discourse in The Book of Mormon:

"And also, ye yourselves will succour those that stand in need of your succour; ye will administer of your substance unto him that standeth in need; and ye will not suffer that the beggar putteth up his petition to you in vain, and turn him out to perish. Perhaps thou shalt say: The man has brought upon himself his misery; therefore I will stay my hand, and will not give unto him of my food, nor impart unto him of my substance that he may not suffer, for his punishments are just— But I say unto you, O man, whosoever doeth this the same hath great cause to repent; and except he repenteth of that which he hath done he perisheth forever, and hath no interest in the kingdom of God. For behold, are we not all beggars?" (Mosiah 4:16-19).

The call to discipleship is a call to service, and far more than Elphaba-like service, but Christlike service. Christ taught us all to love our enemies, and He showed how much he loved even those who nailed Him to the cross, as he died for them and prayed for their forgiveness. Joseph Smith's teachings highlight the need for feelings of love and compassion, rather than judgement and division. On one occasion he taught us about the qualities of the Lord:

But while one portion of the human race are judging and condemning the other without mercy, the great parent of the universe looks upon the whole of the human family with a fatherly care, and paternal regard; he views them as his offspring; and without any of those contracted feelings that influence the children of men, causes

"his sun to rise on the evil and the good; and sends his rain on the just and unjust." He holds the reins of judgment in his hands; he is a wise lawgiver, and will judge all men, -[not according to the narrow contracted notions of men, but]- "according to the deeds done in the body whether they be good or evil; or whether these deeds were done in England, America, Spain, Turkey India... and when the designs of God shall be made manifest, and the curtain of futurity be withdrawn, we shall all of us eventually have to confess, that the Judge of all the earth has done right." (1842).

We should act in a similar way. As I reflect on my service and the expressions of my love I can see that it is easier to show love to those closest to me. If I think about my circles of influence, the closest circle to me is my family, then my friends, other people I know, and then people in the world who may currently be strangers. It is perhaps easier for me to show love to those closer to me, and that the Christlike love I should have is reduced as I work outward. The message of the Gospel of Jesus Christ is that just as Christ showed his love to all, we should be willing to do the same. The heart of our actions as disciples of the Saviour is contained in the Golden Rule:

"Therefore all things whatsoever ye would that men should do to you, do ye even so to them" (Matthew 7:12).

The withholding of our love because of who a person is or their particular circumstance is contrary to the Gospel. We believe in a Heavenly Father who loves each of his children, and in our hearts there should be no division. Joseph Smith was once asked why people followed him as a prophet of the Lord. He replied:

"...it is because I possess the principle of love, all I can offer the world is a good heart and a good hand. The Saints can testify whether I am willing to lay down my life for my brethren. If it has been demonstrated that I have been willing to die for a Mormon, I am bold to declare before heaven that I am just as ready to die in defending the rights of a Presbyterian, a Baptist or a good man of any other denomination; for the same principle which would trample upon the rights of the Latter day Saints would trample upon the rights of the other denomination <Roman Catholics> or of any other denomination who may be unpopular and too weak to defend themselves." (1843-1844).

I love this passage. I spend my life learning and teaching about the religions of the world. As I do this I hope to instil in the people that I teach a respect for others and the realisation that all of our lives are interconnected. This particular teaching was brought home to me one day when I received a knock on my door. It was a couple of people from my local community asking me to sign a petition to stop the building of a Mosque in the local area. How would I have felt if people were protesting the building of a chapel? They left the doorstep without a signature and fully aware that I completely disagreed with their efforts. As members of The Church of Jesus Christ of Latter-day Saints we should be willing to stand for the truth and for human rights, even if it does not directly affect us. As part of our baptismal covenants we promise "to stand as witnesses of God at all times and in all things, and in all places that ye may be in" (Mosiah 18:9).

There is much more to the story of Elphaba, but I think the immediate consequence of her visit to the Emerald City and an audience with the Wizard helps me understand the responsibilities outlined above just a little bit more. Upon meeting with the Wizard she becomes aware that he knows everything that is going on and is actually responsible for the suppression of the Animals. Seeing her passion and power he offers Elphaba a place at his side, which has previously been her dream. While her friend, Glinda encourages her to take on this role, Elphaba realises that she can't sacrifice what she knows to be right for her own ego, power and popularity. As a result of her rejection of the Wizard's offer she is labelled as the 'Wicked Witch' by the Wizard's regime. In an Abinadi-like fashion we must be willing to stand for truth, even if it means standing alone and maybe losing popularity and position. In the long run people will respect us for the integrity that we have in standing for truth. It might be uncomfortable for a while, but we must feel confident to stand in the presence of the Lord. Standing for truth might include standing up for the rights of others, or it might be taking a stand against immorality by walking out of a film.

I have spent quite a lot of time exploring religious themes in Tolkien's writings, and I could go off on many tangents to help have helped me

Some things
I cannot change
But 'til I try,
I'll never know!
Elphaba, Defying Gravity

SAMWISE GAMGEE

understand more about the Gospel of Jesus Christ and my relationship with Him. For example, the food that the Fellowship is called 'Lembas' or 'waybread'. This is bread that sustained the travellers on their journey. It is a direct symbol of the bread of the eucharist (sacrament), in that in the last rites of the Catholic Church the bread that is given is called 'viaticum' or 'bread for the way'. This has caused me to reflect many times on Jesus as the 'bread of life' and how the sacrament can be sustaining on our journey. After that one tangent, I want to focus this part of the booklet on the true hero of The Lord of the Rings: Samwise Gamgee

.

I once spoke at the annual conference of the Tolkien Society. It was a slightly disconcerting experience as I was there in my professional capacity dressed in a shirt and tie, but members of my audience were dressed as Hobbits and as Elves. I always remember this conference with a smile. But I digress. I was part of a panel exploring religion in Middle Earth and one person began their question to me in the following way:

"Thank you for your comments. I think we would all agree that Samwise Gamgee was the true hero of Lord of the Rings. . ."

I was flabbergasted, in conversation with friends I had kept this viewpoint hidden because I thought I was alone in thinking this, yet here I was in a room full of people and it was the majority view. Since that day I have heard many others share similar feelings without denigrating Frodo, Gandalf or Aragorn in any way.

Why do I see Sam as the hero, and what are the things that I can take from his example? Of all of the characters within The Lord of the Rings Sam is the humblest, yet also the most faithful. He begins the tale as a humble gardener, with dreams of Elves and Goblins. He doesn't fall into the adventures by happenstance – because of his bravery and faithfulness he goes into the tasks with his eyes wide open. Indeed, he has never left the Shire before, yet he is faithful in his friendship to Frodo and faces all kinds of adventures and horrors through his living of the virtues that the reader can see within him. Early on he suggests:

"I know we are going to take a very long road, into darkness; but I know I can't turn back. It isn't to see Elves now, nor dragons, nor mountains. . .I have something to do before the end." (Tolkien, (2020 [1954]), p. 88).

He has entered into a course of action that he knows to be right and nothing will dissuade him from that path. Indeed, later in the story when he thinks Frodo is dead, he picks up the ring determined to finish what his friend started. Without too much effort my mind is turned to my journey on the covenant path of the Gospel of Jesus Christ. When I began my journey of the Gospel I "entered in by the gate" (2 Nephi 31:8), and like Sam I was taking a scary step. Just as Sam had never taken one step outside of the Shire, I was entering a new world that promised so much, but was filled with the unknown. I had faith in my Saviour and was ready to "press forward with a steadfastness in Christ, having a perfect brightness of hope, and a love of God and of all men" (2 Nephi 31:20). As I think back over the last thirty years there have been many highs, and some dragons to slay, as I've strived to draw close to the Lord, but as I look at the peace that I can find in my life through the Saviour and the promptings of the Holy Ghost, I am glad that I took that first step and every step since that day.

In some ways it is more than just the journey of living the Gospel, but also the journey of life that we can see in the life of Sam. He leaves the Shire knowing that he must. In so doing he is leaving that which he knows and that which is safe. He endures and succeeds in his journey, but the books close with Sam back in the Shire marrying Rosie and being settled in his life. It is not too much of a stretch to see the journey of Sam to be mortality, after which we return back to live with our Heavenly Father. Life sometimes (maybe oftentimes) is not easy but through the experience of mortality and our relationship with the Saviour we are changed, and we can become what the Lord wants of us. We are often reminded that we are in the process of 'becoming' and we're not there yet.

Trying to explain the purpose of the trials that we go through, two of the early Church Fathers, Augustine and Irenaeus, had different views about the nature of us as humans travelling through mortality and the process of becoming. I will try and explain their views using a stone as a way to show their different understandings. For Augustine, humanity began as a smooth pebble, and as a result of the fall chips and gouges in the stone appeared. The purpose of this life, and the atonement of Christ, is to fill in these chips to make the pebble perfect again. For Irenaeus humanity is created as a pebble with lots of rough edges. As they are rubbed against suffering and battered about these rough edges are smoothed until the smooth pebble is made in the end. I'm not sure which view I think is correct, but I know that all of our lives are designed to help us stand confidently in the presence of God, and to ultimately become perfect, or complete.

Those aspects of Sam's character and his experiences could be enough in helping me understand more about my Gospel living, but this hasn't touched his most important role in the story. There is a further aspect of Sam's journey that highlight his characteristics as a hero. I mentioned before that he became a Ringbearer when he picked up the ring following Frodo's apparent death. While carrying the ring he was tempted with a large garden of his own, but he never gave in to the temptations and the visions which the ring provided. He happily relinquished the ring to Frodo, making him the only being to ever give up the ring both happily and voluntarily (Bilbo had given it up voluntarily but not happily). Such was Sam's lack of ego and also his strength in resisting temptation that for this action alone he can be considered a hero. As I read of Sam's temptations I am reminded of the Saviour in the wilderness:

> ***"Again, the devil taketh him up into an exceeding high mountain, and sheweth him all the kingdoms of the world, and the glory of them; And saith unto him, All these things will I give thee, if thou wilt fall down and worship me. Then saith Jesus unto him, Get thee hence, Satan: for it is written,***

Thou shalt worship the Lord thy God, and him only shalt thou serve" (Matthew 4:8-10).

Neither the Saviour nor Sam succumbed to the temptation of worldly riches. Maybe we can learn from that; there are many things in the world that appear appealing - wealth, popularity and fame to name but three. These are not wrong in themselves, but if we allow them to turn our heads, and to distract us from our relationship with the Lord then they are idols that we have built up unto ourselves (see D&C 1:15-16). The Saviour teaches us that

"Greater love hath no man than this, that a man lay down his life for his friends" (John 15:13)

and while we may not be called to physically lay down our lives, we can lay down our lives in his service. As we do this we are promised joy in this life and eternal life in the world to come

"For whosoever will save his life shall lose it: and whosoever will lose his life for my sake shall find it" (Matthew 16:25).

This does not mean that we spend all of our time fulfilling our Church callings, though they are important. What it does mean is that we place the Saviour at the centre of all that we do, and that we live our lives abiding in Him. This means that we listen for His voice, we stand in His place, and acknowledge Him and His hands in all that we do. We become as the people of King Benjamin:

"And they all cried with one voice, saying: Yea, we believe all the words which thou hast spoken unto us; and also, we know

of their surety and truth, because of the Spirit of the Lord Omnipotent, which has wrought a mighty change in us, or in our hearts, that we have no more disposition to do evil, but to do good continually" (Mosiah 5:2).

It's not that they didn't fail occasionally, it is that their whole disposition, their character, was centred in the Saviour so that they reflected Him in all that they did. Others could see they had "received his image in [their] countenances?" (Alma 5:14).

And in among all of those experiences of Sam, I haven't even mentioned that without him the ring wouldn't have been destroyed.

All things are fulfilled in Jesus Christ

For me every good thing, or good person, points to the Saviour Jesus Christ. I have a friend who feels that emulating the Saviour is too big an ask, and so he looks around and sees people who have Christlike qualities and tries to emulate them, hoping that he will in turn follow Christ. I understand this approach but I'm not really convinced by it. Then again, that is what I have done in this booklet. Ultimately every other hero we may create or place on a pedestal pales in comparison to our Saviour Jesus Christ. He is the only being ever who was without sin, and could say "do as I say, and as I do". President Howard W. Hunter expressed just this thought:

"The world is full of people who are willing to tell us, 'Do as I say.' Surely we have no lack of advice givers on about every subject. But we have so few who are prepared

to say, "Do as I do." And, of course, only One in human history could rightfully and properly make that declaration.

History provides many examples of good men and women, but even the best of mortals are flawed in some way or another. None could serve as a perfect model nor as an infallible pattern to follow, however well-intentioned they might be. Only Christ can be our ideal, our "bright and morning star" (Rev. 22:16). Only he can say without any reservation.

Follow me; learn of me; do the things you have seen me do. Drink of my water and eat of my bread. I am the way, the truth, and the life. I am the law and the light. Look unto me and ye shall live. Love one another as I have loved you" (1994a).

HOPE
CHARITY & LOVE
VIRTUE
KNOWLEDGE
PATIENCE
HUMILITY
DILIGENCE
OBEDIENCE

Each of the heroes I have outlined are fictional, and they all have their foibles. They can serve as useful

OUR SAVIOUR

springboards to help us understand more about the Saviour and how to live His Gospel, but they are not ends in and of themselves. They are useful points of reflection, but are not the subject of our devotion. They can be some of those things in our lives

"which inviteth to do good, and to persuade to believe in Christ" and as such can be seen to be "sent forth by the power and gift of Christ" *(**Moroni 7:16**).*

As I think of the example and characteristics of the Saviour, he is the ultimate exemplar and the hero of heroes. Everything else I encounter should be used to point to Him and the way I should emulate Him in my daily life. Preach My Gospel identifies some of the attributes of the Saviour that I might try and develop in my own life:

FAITH, HOPE, CHARITY & LOVE, VIRTUE, KNOWLEDGE, PATIENCE, HUMILITY, DILIGENCE, OBEDIENCE

It is my responsibility to look for those virtues in my study of the Saviour's life; it is also my opportunity to look for those virtues in the lives of others. Some of those others may be fictional from the worlds of fantasy and science fiction, but many more of those heroes I can find in my relationships with others.

I can see the Christlike attribute of selflessness and charity in the example of my wife, Ruth. I can see the example of diligence in my friends, John and Joanne. I can see humility in the life of someone who I have served with for many years and have grown to love, Bernard. I can see faith and hope in the examples of my children, Eleanor, Abi, Ethan, Gideon and Martha. I can see the patience of the Saviour reflected in the life of Elizabeth, one of the most faithful women know. I can see the Christlike striving for social justice in the example of Blumartha, one of the young women in my ward.

I guess what I'm trying to say, is that wherever we are we can find examples that point us towards Christ and inspire us to be like Him. It's just that in this booklet I have chosen to use examples from fantasy worlds.

Character Synopsis

Superman
Born on the planet Krypton to Jor-El and Lara, with the name of Kal-El. Prior to the destruction of Krypton, his parents sent him to earth to ensure he survived. Found and raised by Jonathan and Martha Kent, with the name Clark. He has many powers including super speed, super strength, x-ray vision and flight. He lives as an adult under the alter-ego as reporter Clark Kent with only a few people knowing his identity as Superman.

The Black Panther/Shuri
The Black Panther identity is bestowed on a member of the Wakandan royal family. Currently the Black Panther is T'Challa following the death of his father. Part of the ceremony to become the Black Panther is the use of a herb to enhance strength and speed to almost superhuman levels. Shuri is T'Challa's younger sister who is rumoured to be taking on the role of the Black Panther in the future.

Elphaba
Elphaba is the name given to the Wicked Witch of the West in the Wizard of Oz. This name is not found in the original book or film. The name is given in the Gregory McGuire book and the musical Wicked. She has an 'interesting' life that leads people to question the use of the word 'wicked' in relation to her.

Samwise Gamgee
In The Lord of the Rings he is introduced as a Hobbit and Frodo's gardener and best friend. Throughout the story he is loyal to Frodo and plays an important role in protecting Frodo and, in the end, destroying the ring.

References

Card, Orson Scott (2010) Orson Scott Card: Different reactions, same book available at https://www.deseret.com/2010/3/25/20104319/orson-scott-card-different-reactions-same-book

Hunter, Howard W. (1994) Church News, June11, 1994

Hunter, Howard W. (1994a) "What Manner of Men Ought Ye to Be?" in Ensign May 1994

Neal A. Maxwell, (1992). "My Servant Joseph" in Ensign May 1992
Maxwell, Neal A. (1992a). "Settle This in Your Hearts" in Ensign November 1992

Pullman, Phillip (2015) My Books available at https://www.philip-pullman.com/newsitem?newsItemID=2

Smith, Joseph (1842) "Times and Seasons, 15 April 1842," p. 759, The Joseph Smith Papers, accessed November 2, 2020, https://www.josephsmithpapers.org/paper-summary/times-and-seasons-15-april-1842/9

Smith, Joseph (1843-1844) "History, 1838–1856, volume E-1 [1 July 1843–30 April 1844]," p. 1666, The Joseph Smith Papers https://www.josephsmithpapers.org/paper-summary/history-1838-1856-volume-e-1-1-july-1843-30-april-1844/36

Tolkien, JRR (2020 [1954]) The Fellowship of the Ring London, UK: Harper Collins

Who is JAMES D. HOLT?

James Holt is Associate Professor of Religious Education at the University of Chester. He is married to Ruth, and they are the parents of four children (now five after a recent wedding). He holds a PhD in Latter-day Saint theology from the University of Chester. He served a mission in the Scotland Edinburgh Mission, and has served as a Bishop, on a stake presidency, and on the Curriculum Writing Committee of the Church for 'Teachings of the Presidents of the Church: Gordon B. Hinckley'.

James is also the author of 'Hearing Him' and has contributed to 'Lenten'.